WHISTLE STOPS
Railway Architecture

Peter Ashley

Everyman Pocket Books
In association with English Heritage

Heaven's gate, Leicester
(p. 1) Glazed terracotta lettering and classical
urns for the Midland Railway in 1892. Take a
look at its companion on p. 80.
Faversham
(p. 2) A freshly painted iron platform gate for a
station originally built for the London Chatham &
Dover Railway in Kent.

Whistle Stops – Railway Architecture

**Published by Everyman Publishers Plc
in association with English Heritage**

© 2001 Everyman Publishers Plc
Text and photographs © Peter Ashley

ISBN 1 84159 045 2

Design by Anikst Design
Printed in Singapore

Everyman Publishers Plc
Gloucester Mansions
140a Shaftesbury Avenue
London WC2H 8HD

contents

introduction The railways were slow in their arrival. The very first, the Stockton to Darlington, was vigorously opposed by Lord Darlington because the proposed route would go through one of his favourite fox covers. But once they did arrive, they changed things forever. Suddenly the industrial revolution powered into top gear, and people's lives and the landscape were irrevocably altered.

At first it was freight, the railways taking on the roads and canals as the prime mover of goods. The possibilities of passenger traffic soon became apparent, and from the first journeys that merely adopted stagecoach practices, where tickets were sold at local inns, a network of lines and stations rapidly spread into every community. Fuelled by a mania that has distinct parallels with our own dot.com revolution, railway companies were quickly established and, as with all commercial ventures, a fight for survival followed. The fittest prevailed, gobbling up the weak in an orgy of amalgamations.

The social consequences were immense. From the first smoky jaunts for the rich, the railway became a facility for everyone, and most places in England could be reached within a day. Commercial travellers seized opportunities, pleasure seekers thumbed gazetteers, businessmen pocketed season tickets, and soldiers whistled off to war. Queen Victoria became the first royal to travel by train in 1842, and John Tawell the first murderer to be apprehended by the railway's electric telegraph in 1845.

The landscape changed, sometimes subtly, sometimes with dramatic effect, as railway engineers became pioneers. Brunel plotted the course of the Great Western, becoming lost for days in the wilds of Wiltshire trying to find his fellow surveyors, and Stephenson took giant leaps of faith with his multi-arched viaducts and cavernous tunnels. Far too much of this incredible infrastructure, where no village in England was more than 12 miles from a station, has disappeared. The green humps of old track beds cross fields, looking like prehistoric extra-long barrows, and ornamented disused stations, robbed now of their leaded windows, have become homes with maintenance-free double glazing.

The 21st century sees what we hope is the dawning of a new age, where this irreplaceable legacy of architecture and engineering is now being appreciated, restored and reused. Railtrack are creating the conditions for a railway renaissance by the sensitive restoration of the architecture within their system; preserved steam railway lines meticulously recreate past glories; and English Heritage care as much for country stations as they do for their castles and abbeys. Each year they recommend more buildings for listing, often after they are drawn to their attention by historical societies, local authorities and, very importantly, members of the public. Without *your* support and commitment, many of the remarkable things you will see on this whistle-stop tour would be lost or damaged.

This book represents a limited journey around England, with the inevitable result that some favourites may be missing. I hope that the inclusion of perhaps less celebrated but equally rewarding locations will help to compensate, and in any case, there is so much to enjoy that a second book is already being considered. The main aim, as with the other volumes in this series, is to whet the appetite. At the risk of sounding like a 19th-century religious tract, use it as a key to discover the glories and riches of this unique part of our history.

stations

No more will I go to Blandford Forum and Mortehoe
On the slow train from Midsomer Norton and Mumby Road
No churns, no porter, no cat on a seat
At Chorlton-cum-Hardy or Chester-le-Street.
'The Slow Train' by Michael Flanders and Donald Swann

Individual railway stations are like churches; scenes of joyous arrivals and sad departures, both are about peoples' lives more than simply examples of magnificent architecture. Mumby Road in Lincolnshire was a personal favourite from my childhood. Now I know that it was on the Louth, Mablethorpe and Willoughby Loop; its weather-boarded platform buildings had decorative bargeboards, and the walls of the station house were hung with red tiles. All this passed me by in the early 50s as I looked out for the dark blue station sign, its white letters telling me the holiday had begun. The tracks have long disappeared, and all the buildings except the station house – a sad tale that was repeated with dreadful monotony all over the country.

Now, the surviving 19th-century splendours are emerging from long years of grime and soot; Wellingborough looks more than ever like a row of ornamental estate cottages, and Grange-over-Sands once again flaunts its celebratory seaside air.

Settle, North Yorkshire This is the first taste of the 'Derby Gothic' stations to come as the Settle to Carlisle line sets off across fell and dale, facing 72 miles of difficult country and unpredictable weather. Local stone is outlined with white barge-boards on the gable ends, and Midland Railway crimson lake paint is liberally applied to everything else.

Hertford East, Hertfordshire Restoration has brought back the full impact of Hertford East. With its dramatic arched entrances, pinnacles, parapets and a louvred cupola, the building echoes Tudor and Jacobean styles in red brick, stone and terracotta. W.N. Ashbee brought all this together for the Great Eastern Railway in 1888. A perfect station for this Hertfordshire county town.

> **Bristol Temple Meads** A French Gothic tower dominates Bristol Temple Meads, a wonderful confection of battlements and pinnacles in variegated stone. Sir Matthew Digby Wyatt made the tower the crowning glory of his new frontage, completed in 1878, which also boasts an intricate canopy in iron and glass to frame the entrance.

> **Southend-on-Sea, Essex** Southend-on-Sea owes its considerable success to the railway. One of three stations, Southend Victoria brings commuters and day-trippers to and from London Liverpool Street. Designed for the Great Eastern Railway by W.N. Ashbee, it retains his regard for 'Jacobethan' detailing with stone mullioned windows and hammerbeam canopy supports.

York The arching curve of William Peachey's iron roof culminates in these magnificent glazed end-screens. The atmosphere here is still one of shrill Acme Thunderer whistles blowing, with billows of steam rising nearly 50 feet to the roof top. The spandrels of the supporting brackets still proudly bear the multicoloured heraldry of the North Eastern Railway.

Grange-over-Sands, Cumbria This Italianate station, built in 1877 for the Furness Railway, clings to the shoreline of Morecambe Bay. It forms part of a perfect Victorian seaside group with the Grange Hotel, whose design it copies, and the carefully tended shrubberies and lawns connecting them. The restoration of the station, with its hipped roofs and glass awnings, was an early example of Railtrack's regeneration programme.

Kemble, Gloucestershire Kemble is an 1872 Tudor-style station dressed in warm Cotswold stone. The seats still have the evocative GWR symbol cast in the supports. The giant water tank is in cast iron, supported by six circular columns, and was originally fed by a natural spring discovered when the station was built. It supplied the GWR works in Swindon as well as the village.

Wellingborough, Northamptonshire C.H. Driver's 1857 red brick Wellingborough has all the hallmarks of the Midland Railway's penchant for the cottage style. The coloured brick dressings, slate roofs and arched lozenge-glazed windows give a warm, homely feel. The supports for the glazed platform awnings are crammed with cast-iron vegetation.

∧ **Market Harborough, Leicestershire** A Queen Anne house masquerading as a railway station. The Midland Railway converged with the London & North Western here at Market Harborough, and a new station was required to serve them both. The style was enjoying a fashionable revival in 1884, and the red brick and stone pilasters combine well with the elegant dormer and chimney stacks.

> **Stamford, Lincolnshire** At first, Stamford refused to have the railway anywhere near it. When it did finally arrive, the Tudor manor architecture became an heraldic trumpet for this outstanding stone-built town. Built for the Syston & Peterborough Railway by Sancton Wood, it was taken over by the Midland before the opening in 1848, but 'SPR' remains cut out of the weathervane flashing in the wind on top of the octagonal turret. This elegant limestone building still proudly catches the light, now crowded by a housing estate built over the old coalyards.

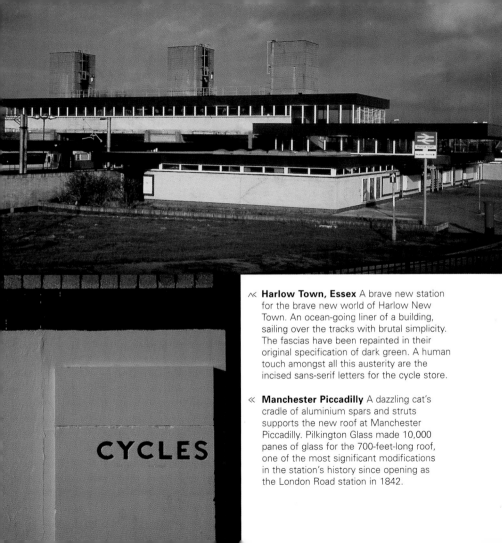

CYCLES

Harlow Town, Essex A brave new station for the brave new world of Harlow New Town. An ocean-going liner of a building, sailing over the tracks with brutal simplicity. The fascias have been repainted in their original specification of dark green. A human touch amongst all this austerity are the incised sans-serif letters for the cycle store.

Manchester Piccadilly A dazzling cat's cradle of aluminium spars and struts supports the new roof at Manchester Piccadilly. Pilkington Glass made 10,000 panes of glass for the 700-feet-long roof, one of the most significant modifications in the station's history since opening as the London Road station in 1842.

Kings Cross, London The Gothic shadow of the St Pancras clock tower falls across the functional simplicity of London's King's Cross. Lewis Cubitt built the terminus of the Great Northern Railway here in 1846-50, the profile of the two round-arched roofs reflected in the glazing on the plain yellow brick frontage, divided in the centre by an Italianate clock tower. John Betjeman said: 'Of all London's termini Kings Cross is the least pretentious. It is an engineering job.'

Liverpool Street, London Here is a perfect marriage of old and new. The 1991 twin towers at Liverpool Street pose like a minster in the heart of the City of London, (Southwell in Nottinghamshire comes to mind), part of a massive refurbishment of the station. Yellow stock East Anglian bricks reflect the destinations flagged up on the glittering glass and steel concourse inside.

St. Pancras, London The Midland Railway were determined to announce their presence in London with a style guaranteed to bring gulps of astonishment to passengers and competitors alike. The actual station is a tour-de-force glass and iron trainshed, built on pillared vaults designed precisely to take Burton beer barrels. Most people's perception of St. Pancras, however, will be the soaring turreted frontage, formerly the Midland Grand Hotel on the Euston Road. The best materials from the shires realised Sir Gilbert Scott's design in 1868-74: Gripper's patent Nottingham brick, Ancaster, Mansfield and Ketton stone, grey and red granite. A first-class hotel for the Victorian traveller – sadly at present only a first-class film location.

Staverton, Devon The South Devon Railway follows the River Dart down from Buckfastleigh to Totnes. Staverton is typical of the vast number of small stations on country branch lines that served as focal points in rural communities. Here at Staverton is a freeze-frame image of how we'd like it all still to be: milk churns line up on their trolley, enamelled signs announce Fry's Chocolate and Spiller's Shapes, and a Royal Daylight oil wagon and GWR camping coach sleep in the sidings.

Rothley, Leicestershire Here in Rothley is a reminder of the vision of Sir Edward Watkin to create a fast route across England, from Manchester and Sheffield into London and on to the continent by a channel tunnel. Viaducts flew across smoky Midland towns, and the first train arrived at Marylebone in 1899. In less than 70 years most of it had gone. Here in the fields of Leicestershire a section of the Great Central Railway is carefully preserved. Rothley Station has all the authentic detail, with an amply proportioned porters' trolley left next to a name board that doubles up as a poster hoarding, a covered stairway to the entrance on the overbridge, and a robust example of a boldly lettered coalyard store.

valances One of the most distinctive features of railway stations are the decorative wooden valances attached to the leading edge of platform canopies. Their purpose was simple: to deflect wind and rain, and of course, smoke and steam away from waiting passengers. The sheer variety of fretworked patterns is astonishing – over 200 in the south east alone. Here is just a sample ...

Sleaford, Lincolnshire

∧ **Thetford, Norfolk**
> **Great Malvern, Worcestershire**
≫ **Faversham, Kent**

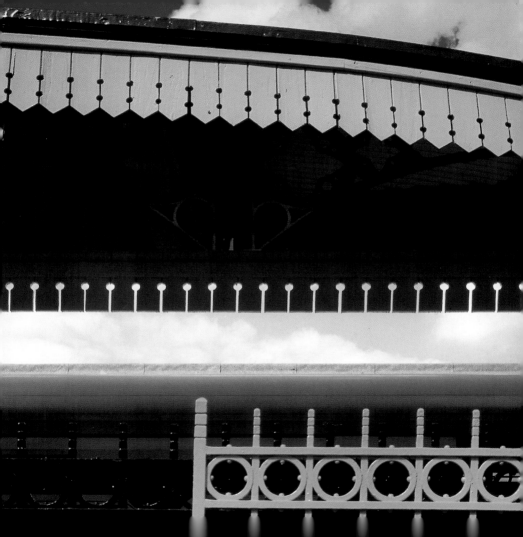

clocks Before the railway age, time was a fairly vague concept, marked for most people by church clocks. Telling the time was a local issue and accuracy was of no consequence when one village's clock told a different time to the next. Allowances were easily made even by stagecoach passengers finding that Plymouth was 20 minutes behind London. The running of a railway, however, meant having a consistent timetable, but not until the advent of the electric telegraph did it become possible for Greenwich Mean Time to be adopted nationally. Public clocks suddenly appeared everywhere, particularly at railway stations. Prominent timekeepers were hung over platforms and up amongst the decorations of pigeon-haunted clock towers. So much so that GMT became in common speech 'railway time'.

≪ **Bath Spa**
< **Eastbourne**

signalling and crossings

signalling and crossings If you were asked to draw a signal box, it would probably conform to a design developed over 70 years from the 1860s. Although there are obvious exceptions, the accepted image of a signal box is still of a glazed and pitch-roofed operational deck with levers linked to a locking room underneath. There may be decorative barge boards on the eaves, almost certainly a stove, and hopefully a little brick-built lavatory. They will bristle with multicoloured levers, mahogany block instruments with twitching indicators, and obligatory kettles. They may also be the only place where it's still possible to see the lettering styles of past railway companies in enamel and wood. In 1900 there were 13,000 boxes, now there are fewer than 1,000, but fortunately many of them are quite rightly listed buildings.

Lincoln, East Holmes Once set amongst the warehouses of Brayford Pool in Lincoln, East Holmes is a Great Northern box from around 1873. Now standing alone on the banks of the Witham, this October day saw the Red Arrows from RAF Scampton give an aerial salute.

> **Coombe Junction, Cornwall** This wooden hut, finished in GWR chocolate and cream, houses a token instrument that thoughtfully allows only one train at a time on a single line.

>> **Culgaith, Cumbria** Heavy leverage at Culgaith catching the last of the sun on the Settle to Carlisle line. Set on a hillside above the River Eden, this 1908 box is passed just before trains enter the 661-yard-long Culgaith Tunnel.

> **Darley Dale, Derbyshire**
> The preservation of closed lines has
> resulted in the restoration of many
> boxes. This superb example, painted in
> Midland livery, is on Peak Rail's line at
> Darley Dale.

> **Culgaith** See previous page.

>> **St. James Deeping, Lincolnshire**
> This yellow brick and exuberantly
> barge-boarded box was built for the
> Great Northern Railway in 1876, and
> is still in daily use on the Peterborough
> to Spalding line.

>>> **Lincoln, High Street** Shoppers in
> Lincoln have the pleasure of coming out
> of one shop, and before going into the
> next, having to wait for 60 oil tankers to
> hammer by in front of their noses; a
> living, breathing railway in the centre of
> town. The 1874 High Street box is almost
> in the churchyard of St. Mary le Wigford.

>>> **Oakham, Rutland** A simple 1899
> Midland box by a level crossing, but
> one with a place in the history of railway
> modelling; it was the prototype for an
> Airfix plastic construction kit.

Brundall, Norfolk A footbridge for the impatient next to the original oil lamp and gate at Brundall, east of Norwich.

Wansford, Cambridgeshire A long cabin built in 1907 to serve the LNWR. It now presides over the preserved Nene Valley Railway line that runs from Yarwell through Wansford station to Peterborough.

Grosmont, North Yorkshire Semaphore signals on the North Yorkshire Moors Railway, one of the longest preserved lines in the country.

bridges and viaducts

Bridges appear in almost countless forms, from Brunel's iron tubes on the breathtaking Royal Albert bridge at Saltash, to the passenger-friendly cream and green footbridge at Ropley on the Watercress Line in Hampshire. Everywhere a river or a road needed to be crossed, designers and engineers produced an extraordinary variety of solutions.

The distinction between a bridge and a viaduct can often get blurred, but for our purposes here a viaduct is a way of crossing a valley on a succession of towering arches. Their sheer power is often lost on the train passenger, who is aware, if of anything at all, only of the ground beneath the track suddenly dropping away for a few seconds. From below they are the friendly local monsters striding over fields and rooftops.

Kingsferry Bridge, Swale, Kent This is the only crossing point between the Isle of Sheppey and the rest of Kent. These gigantic croquet hoops support a vertical lift bridge that carries both road and rail over the muddy reaches of the River Swale. It is raised by an engineer hiding in one of the piers to allow shipping in and out of Ridham Dock, and for yachtsmen who display a bucket on their masts.

Blackfriars, London Thameslink trains cross the river into Blackfriars Station on five wrought-iron arches. Originally called St. Paul's Railway Bridge, after the former name of the station, it was designed in 1884-86 by J. Wolfe Barry and H.M. Brunel. The eye, however, is inevitably drawn to the remains of Cubitt and Turner's bridge of 1862-64. The spans have gone, leaving deep pink Romanesque columns rising up out of the water. Even more spectacular is the brilliantly coloured insignia of the London, Chatham & Dover Railway, a proud Victorian badge built into the redundant pylon on the southern abutment. The chimney in the background first served the magnificent Bankside Power Station, now metamorphosed into Tate Modern.

The low-lying land surrounding the rivers and Broads between Norwich and the coast necessitated swing bridges that enabled passage for river traffic. Several survive, still in daily use, and fly their red flags in the Broadland breeze to warn boats that bridges are likely to swing across their bows. Somerleyton and Reedham bridges span not only their respective rivers but the county boundary between Norfolk and Suffolk.

« **Somerleyton, Suffolk** The ten-minute wait indicator board is displayed to boats as an afternoon train from Lowestoft to Norwich crosses the Waveney. Notice the wooden vaulting horse at the back of the box.

∧ **Reedham, Norfolk** A Lowestoft-bound train crosses the River Yare at watery Reedham. Road traffic must turn upstream to a little chain ferry amongst the reeds, the only crossing between Norwich and Great Yarmouth.

< **Oulton near Lowestoft, Suffolk** Lake Lothing is separated from Oulton Broad by a narrow channel spanned by this swing bridge. The graceful effect of the iron girders is only slightly spoiled by the operator's wooden hut hanging precariously over the side.

Royal Albert Bridge, Saltash, Cornwall
The Royal Albert Bridge spans the Tamar
between Devon and Cornwall. Brunel's name
is proudly displayed on the portals of what is
the only railway-carrying suspension bridge in
the country. He spanned the river with two
gigantic wrought-iron tubes, floated into
position on pontoons with much semaphore
flag waving. They were then lifted onto the
stone piers in front of a hushed audience of
thousands on the banks. After its opening by
Prince Albert in 1859, the seriously ill engineer
was taken over the bridge lying on a bed in an
open-topped carriage.

Balcombe, West Sussex Deep in the Sussex countryside a gentle river meanders its way through a wooded valley. In 1840 the London and Brighton Railway transformed the scene forever with one of the most impressive viaducts in the country. Flying 92 feet over the River Ouse valley on 37 brick arches, the entrances are guarded by eight Italianate pavilions.

< **Knaresborough, North Yorkshire** The Knaresborough Viaduct spans the River Nidd on four broad arches. The foundations were sunk into the sandstone in 1848 for the Leeds & Thirsk Railway, and it now appears totally absorbed into the landscape. Trains suddenly and unexpectedly appear as if by magic from between the houses.

∧ **Welland Valley, Rutland** A wintry sun lights January flood water and the Welland Valley Viaduct, joining Northamptonshire with Rutland. Thousands of sheepskins were laid on boggy ground to soak up moisture before construction could start. The 82 brick arches cost £1,000 each in 1879, and outside of surburban London this is the longest (1,275 yards) viaduct on the railway system.

Ruswarp, North Yorkshire The Bridge Inn at Ruswarp celebrates the road crossing of the River Esk, and the simple lattice truss railway bridge at its side slips by almost unnoticed. It is typical of thousands of unsung bridges that do sterling service over the system.

Hastings, East Sussex Heavily fluted Doric columns carry a wrought-iron girder bridge over Queens Road in Hastings. The columns are formed from tubes in rare cast iron, a material discouraged after Stephenson's Dee Bridge in Chester collapsed in 1847. This is one of the earliest railway bridges, built in 1851 for the South Eastern Railway.

Bath, North East Somerset Soon after leaving Bath Spa, the London to Bristol line crosses a 28-arch viaduct, and now neatly positioned in the middle of a roundabout on the Lower Bristol Road are these turreted abutments, for all the world like the entrance to a medieval abbey. The sure touch of Isambard Kingdom Brunel ensured the sympathy of his railway with the stones of Georgian Bath.

›› **Wilmcote, Warwickshire** Repainted in the original light and dark stone colours, this covered footbridge also features an 1883 GWR monogram. The instructions to use it are still there in bold cast-iron letters.

›› **Ropley, Hampshire** The footbridge at Ropley on the Mid Hants 'Watercress' line. It is painted in the Southern Railway's light stone colour and their ubiquitous mid-chrome green, retained for most metal fittings including signs, lamp posts, drain pipes and railings.

details Railway architecture is often richly embellished and enlivened by decorative detail and incidental additions. Beauty can arise directly out of function, as on the staircases at Exeter St. Davids and Grantham, and little unexpected delights appear everywhere, such as the original W.H.Smith sign still hanging (at the time of photography at least) at Hull Paragon.

Horsted Keynes Everything for an emergency on the Bluebell Line in Sussex.

> **Oakham, Rutland**
  Swirling canopy supports

> **Radlett, Hertfordshire**
  Delicious cast-iron plums

» **Ulverston, Cumbria**
  Dark red sandstone and
  Italianate features surrounding
  a doorway

»» **Hull Paragon, East Yorkshire**
  An original W.H.Smith
  'Newsboy' vitreous enamel sign

»» **Grantham, Lincolnshire**
  Freshly painted cast-iron
  lozenges on a staircase

∧ Supporting stars at **Scarborough**

> **Exeter St. Davids** in Devon
> has glorious balustrades on the staircases,
> patterns redolent of locomotive connecting
> rods in green, cream and gold.

∧ **Horsted Keynes, Sussex**
Travellers' fare

> **Nottingham**
Art-Nouveau lily pads gilding
a gate

≫ **Great Malvern, Worcestershire**
Iron flora

tunnels There are officially 1,049 tunnels in Britain. Most are stupendous feats of engineering, boring directly into the physical obstacles to a direct route, avoiding lengthy and circuitous diversions. The traditional method of construction was to sink trial holes from which tunnelling commenced in opposing directions. On completion these shafts often became the tunnel ventilators, and at one time you could stand in a field and watch while a steam train sent out a puff of smoke as it passed underneath. In the early days of railway engineering there were very genuine fears of passengers suffocating, and tunnels were built high and wide, often with enormous ventilators, like Stephenson's brick castles at Kilsby in Northamptonshire.

« **Clayton Tunnel, East Sussex** The Clayton Tunnel on the London to Brighton line has always attracted attention because of the house perched precariously between the turrets. It may have been built as the home of the railway worker responsible for the gas that originally lit the tunnel. Engineered by J.U. Rastrick, the tunnel was opened for the London & Brighton Railway in 1841.

‹ **Box Tunnel, Wiltshire** This is the western portal of Brunel's Box Tunnel in Wiltshire. Its construction involved 4,000 men and 300 horses working around the clock by candlelight, burning a ton of candles every week for two and a half years. For a considerable time after the opening in 1841, some passengers were afraid to travel through what was then the longest tunnel ever built (1,452 yards). They would hire horses in either Corsham or Bath to ride over the hill. Legend has it that the rising sun shines through the tunnel on only one day a year – Brunel's birthday.

< A blue-brick tunnel ventilator alone in the fields near **Glaston, Rutland**

∧ A stone ventilator down on the farm at Howley Hall in Yorkshire, one of three serving the **Morley Tunnel**

> Railway buffs next to one of Stephenson's crenallated **Kilsby Tunnel** ventilators. They can be seen on both sides of the A5 in Northamptonshire; the earth mounds are spoil from the tunnel excavation.

acknowledgements

Many of the photographs first appeared in a limited edition book commissioned by Railtrack PLC, and it is to them that I am most grateful for their unstinting help and support both for that edition and for continuing help on 'Whistle Stops'. In particular I would like to thank Kathy Thomas, Gill Hacking and Clive Brandon. At English Heritage I am indebted to Val Horsler and Simon Bergin for listening to me ran on about this series for four years.

Thanks are due to countless individuals who helped me on my journeys: station staff, signalmen, crossing keepers, farmers (with and without shotguns), and the unswerving interest in my work by my friends at Kilsby Tunnel. At Everyman: David Campbell, Clémence Jacquinet and Sandra Pisano. For brilliant design and infinite patience: Anikst Design. Rupert Farnsworth for beer and sometimes helpful comments and Elizabeth Raven-Hill for just about everything else.

The extract from 'The Slow Train' is from The Songs of Michael Flanders and Donald Swann. Copyright the estate of Michael Flanders and Donald Swann. By permission.

bibliography

The Railway Heritage of Britain Gordon Biddle & O.S. Nock, Michael Joseph 1983. The Oxford Companion to British Railway History Edited by Jack Simmons and Gordon Biddle, Oxford University Press 1997. The Buildings of England Series Penguin Books. The Shell County Guides, Faber & Faber. Signal Boxes Michael A. Vanns, Ian Allan 1997. Country Railways Paul Atterbury & Ian Burgum, Weidenfeld & Nicolson 1996. GWR Country Stations Chris Leigh Ian Allan, 1981. Railway Liveries 1923-1947 Brian Haresnape Ian Allan 1989. Settle & Carlisle Michael Pearson, J.M.Pearson & Son 1998. London's Historic Railway Stations John Betjeman & John Gay, John Murray 1972. The Railways of Britain Past and Present O.S.Nock, Batsford 1949.

Stansted Airport, Essex Stansted became London's third airport with the opening of a new complex designed by Sir Norman Foster. The station is underneath the main terminal, and from here passengers are taken on purpose-built tracks that connect with the main line into London Liverpool Street.